More Advance Praise for *Tarnish and Masquerade*

"These sunwashed revelations — this lilting, uproarious, precise gospel — brings so much to the table that the reader is nearly overwhelmed. Roger Bonair-Agard is his own revolution, a deft purveyor of unflinching politics, stark sensuality and the relentless drum of the island home that beckons from every page. There is simply no resisting these stanzas, absolutely no way to turn away from what they will do to you."

— Patricia Smith, author of *Life According to Motown; Big Town, Big Talk; Close to Death* and *Teahouse of the Almighty*

"In *Tarnish and Masquerade*, Roger Bonair-Agard attempts to render a history of love and indignation. The collection begins in a backyard of Trinidad, and traces (through gaelle and underworld and prank and Brooklyn) a music of steel-drum tri-tones, a rage both historical and intimate, and a joy entangled in — and excavated out of — one man's wanderings and witness, his enigmatic sense of home. Perhaps you have heard some of these poems in Bonair-Agard's own detonating tenor, bounding off the walls, gutting the space of its silences. Become familiar again with those poems. Read them yourself aloud. You may hear your own voice transformed. You may not recognize the sound. It is your English, riled and rechristened in the bardic carnivals of heat, laughter, and calypso."

— Patrick Rosal, author of *Uprock Headspin Scramble and Dive* and *My American Kundiman*

"Roger Bonair-Agard's careful mix of resistance, pride, regret and joy is a resonant hymn to the exile. These strong, full-hearted poems describe the longing for home and tradition in a land with people and problems not of one's own making; reading them is a dance with rhythm and desire."

— Daphne Gottlieb, author of *Why Things Burn* and *Final Girl*

Tarnish and *Masquerade*

Roger Bonair-Agard

Cypher Books, a Division of Rattapallax
New York, New York

Cypher Books, a Division of Rattapallax
532 La Guardia Place, Suite 353
New York, NY 10012 USA
info@rattapallax.com / www.cypherbooks.com

Cover design by Hamid Rahmanian
Cover photograph by Kristine Gottilla
Author photo by Peter Dressel
Cypher logo design by Kenny Kiernan
CD mastering by Fred Stesney

ISBN: 1-892494-69-8
ISBN: 978-1-892494-69-6

Library of Congress Catalog Card Number: 2006923059

These poems have previously appeared in the following literary journals
and anthologies:

"cane brulee" (*Cave Canem Summer Retreat Anthology*)
"Mandate" (*National Poetry Slam Anthology*)
"Dorothy Coming Down" (*Caribbean Living Magazine*)
"Bird Watching" (*Rattapallax 11*)
"naming and other Christian things" (*Burning Down the House: Selected
Poems from the Nuyorican Poets Cafe's National Poetry Slam Champions*)

First Edition: 2006

For
Hyacinth Bonair-Agard
and Jamil Agard
who continue to hold me

Contents

ACT ONE

could believe dis ting?   3
chantuel hymns   5
cane brulee   8
Mandate   10
The devil in music   12
Melda's song   16
Dorothy coming down   20

ACT TWO

what the water gave me   25
seahorses   26
unplanned / gift   28
in the same breath as my father   29
photo graph   31
Bullet Points   32
armed into the night   35
Waiting for Carla   36

ACT THREE

Lay me Down
    Venus Asleep (Oil on Canvas) b. Paul Delvaux   42
To Kali   43
phantom limbs   45
blue sex prodigy   46
America: 1878 - called   48

ACT FOUR

we come far   53
The future of America in the belly of the beast
    (the millennium edition)   57
song for Trent Lott (who said we'd be a better country
    today if Strom Thurman had won the presidency)   61
Bird Watching   64
first thoughts of a come-again messiah when informed
    of the protocol of the new crucifixions   67
Truth applies for a green card   70
For John Hollander   71

ACT FIVE
Spring   75
how the ghetto loves us back   77
everything comes together – saga of a ghetto
 neighborhood   80
naming and other Christian things   85
The sadness of migration   88

Tarnish and *Masquerade*

Act One

"who so foolish, eh?
to actually leave de promise' lan'
and go somewhere dem know
is pure struggle pure ketch-arse
say dey lookin' fuh better life –
who rich in dem own lan'
an' for spite look fuh poverty
in nex' man own? yuh could
believe dis chupidness?
yuh could believe dis ting?"

chantuel hymns

I lost my virginity   to calypso
        to the songs of slaves
        the ghosts of souls
        that disappear with languages lost

my grandfather's French-African patois
  never sang to me
  his 'talk some — keep some' philosophy
meant swallow   all your pride
none of his chantuel hymns
or 'oui papa'
except through these songs — L'Ouverture's dream
rhyming its way hard
through steel pan and the repartee of African ballad
griot story made freedom song

my waist learned to move
  with the whip   with the song   with the prayer
  with the silent acquiescence of my grandfather's tongue
phasing out his own Creole
for the Victorian flourish of his father's hand
through the ghost of a language lost
learned the stroke of a sweet fuck
a soul taking up residence in a music
surviving life as a squatter in a redeemed people's songs

I lost my virginity
  to the echo and crackle of the cane brulee
first declaration of emancipation
bacchanalian festival
turned revolt   turned African turned lost tongue
turned the still raging fire
hollowing out the soul of the oil drum
to revive Africa as a stubborn tenant
in a European mask

We learned how to fuck like this
 this 'sweet wine'
like surreptitious   like uprising
like make more Africans while massa sleep
  make more drums to replace the ones banned
more tongues to sing the ones cut out
and made to flop useless
on the cocoa floor – the tongue
my grandfather replaced with the black foot dance
of the coffee bean
and the bois of the gayelle
and the future for his children
and the land that he left

This is how we learn to move
  slow figure eight from waist down
  put the heartbeat into the grind
and J'ouvert and Dimanche Gras
    we learn to move like sand
  shift like the chatter of forbidden tongues
Shango-Baptiste et Creole Francais
La Reine Riviere and the lifetimes
of movement in Bourg Mulatresse and Laventille
and all that is Africa in Trinidad
   from the slave barracks in Belmont
   to the burial grounds in Point Fortin

Land on our shores
fascinated by our insouciant rhythms
or the movement of waistlines through impossible emotions
and remember these are tongues
these are lost languages
these are the dozens   this is tap dance
   through steelpan and calypso

We learned to live
under the shadows
of our grandfathers' tongues
  in the shade of the immortelle
  in the middle of the night
  in the stomp of Shango ritual
  in the silence of Ash Wednesday
  in the chaos of Savannah dust
  in love and lust
   and the eternal stroking of our hips
  we learned to move
we learned to move
we learned to move
  and still we have the language to prove it

cane brulee

In the backyard   peas   two kinds of thyme
a lime tree a sorrell bush paw paw passion fruit
two mango trees one avocado tree
and a patch of cane   flowering brilliant
to every sense   even touch is heightened
in the swelling of fertility

the smells haunt summer
pungent turn of coffee beans drying in wait
for their feet for the blue-black wash
all the way to ankles as they dance for turning

his brother crawling across the porch
watching them laughing

the cilantro attaching itself to the memories
of flowers and staying on for dinner
he would track the rancor
of a dead congoree through the house
from his sojourns through the bush
to the fresh-cut grass of the savannah

these are the smells he will remember
when he first makes love they will
lift him up call him to passion
the way the smell of a woman's skin
will call him to her

interrupt the intricate six-eighths timing
he imagines his heartbeat
will call him to improvise prayer
on his lips   and rain   smells like rain
like the distance between the splash
of droplets on hot asphalt

the smell of women will undo him
this summer re-invent the topography
of his becoming

schoolyard fights
cruel humor on his sleeves
the same cutthroat instinct as musk
and shield

where the madness will start
where he will bi-polarize
into the ghosts of his histories

where he will learn power
that the ability to step on something
is the only thing that prevents
him from being stepped on

where he will learn to drink rum
worrying about clothes
gain control of his body in dance

this summer of smells
and salvation   of all things coming together
the summer when his brother will learn
to walk and he will first make love

somehow the conflagration saves him
because all he can see in his brother
is light   all he can see in this woman
is his reflection   he will dance the coffee

with his father one last time the beans
will turn   fill the air with scent heavy
as song his brother will go everywhere
wtth him and the map of love he will
become could lead him to everything

9

Mandate

(after Patrick Rosal)

To laugh at weaker boys (or at least the less sharp-tongued)
    to kick ball till the moon rose
    or something vital bled — we lived
To wait like predator
    for the first note of a slow jam
    to grind ourselves into the wall
    with a pretty girl between us
    and make sure our boys were watching

We were tropical suave post-colonial oil money fellows
and we had to do well — in all things
    in Latin
    in the First Queen's Royal College Scout band
    in talking shit
    and especially in football
so we practiced memorizing where
our defenders were
so we could look the other way
as we went past them
cuz it was only cool
if you made it seem effortless

we were sophisticates like that
looking for immortality in the tales of others
and most of our friends were still alive

To buy two sno-cones from George
    whose rickety cart parked outside
    the school each day
To have the cones stacked with extra syrup and condensed milk
To gather around the cart
    because George always had sensible shit to say
To follow that with the hottest spiciest
    doubles from the doubles-man behind the cafeteria
    who built two multi-level homes
    off the profits from our purchases
To laugh at that irony

To pick on the faggot boys
  because we wanted our fathers to think we were men

To join the new dance-craze revolution
To stop traffic on Frederick Street
  just to see Doc Scientist and Froggie
  spin on vinyl pop-lock head-stand
  electric-boogie dead-man

To sit on the steps
  of the downtown shopping plaza
  and stare at the beauty of our women
To believe at sixteen
  that they were our women

To welcome satellite TV and music videos
  like it was God
  because who can see the future anyway
  It was 1984
and we were busy looking good
mimicking everything we saw

To go watch Gip play better than the rest of us
to see him collect the ball on the outside
of his left foot count the on-rushing defender's footsteps
and slide the ball deftly through his legs
while looking the other way
  effortless like that

Our bodies hadn't begun to betray us yet
Kirk and Gregory and Rudy and Peter were still alive
Dave still had his legs
and the worst thing wasn't not doing well
It was seeming   like you were trying too hard

The devil in music

— for Wammo and the North Stand

They say they want to have a musical change in pan
Well I didn't tell them Yes
Well I didn't tell them No

Lord Kitchener (from 'Pan in A Minor')

I'm telling the Texan
of the phenomenon of Pan in A Minor
100-piece orchestras of oil drums
harmonizing the songs of slaves
with the twelve notes of the Western scale
in unheard-of tonics and chords

see us grin together
acknowledge the goose bumps
as I explain the baptismal swell
of savannah dust blooming
like babies' breath amongst the bouquet
of 100 pan men 4 flag women
and a moko jumbie

soak in the ego of my own description
as if that is the source of his joy
pretend I am not a man
lost in the land of another
pretend I am not telling my friend of this
as much to keep the memories fresh
as to share this pound of flesh
that hurts more and more every day
I move further away from home

as if my removal from the land
of cascadoo and las' lap mas'
is not itself a tearing of flesh
that neither me nor country is healed from

like my tattoos aren't a scarification ritual
that reminds me I'm alive
the ink one big blue-black mark
where Arouca where Cascade where the Savannah
where Trinidad was ripped from me

the Texan is laughing now
as he tries to picture the bass man
spinning like a rooster in a gayelle
negotiating the six-drum of bass
laughing as he tries to mimic
something he has never seen
100 men jumping in unison
as they make music
as they pogo like Masai
through the diminished fifth
and the moko jumbie man is raised
to a fever of exultation

and it is 3 AM and the Texan
might as well not be listening
because I am shirtless and prancing
and for five minutes Renegades are on stage
making Jit look like the genius he is again
and a woman in the tightest shorts
between her and her God
and a gold tooth to the front
is offering a heaping plate of pelau
from a basket to wash down the full cup
of hot rum in my hand
and the man still stemming
the blood from his temple from the bottle
thrown there half hour ago
is smiling again

and for five minutes the Texan
is jubilant background noise
and this muggy Brooklyn summer
this four-story walk-up
this fire escape and the gunshots in the distance
are somebody's cruel idea of a joke

and me and Trinidad are whole again
no wounds between us
no IMF debt
no West Indies losing to England
or Australia or India at cricket

me and Trinidad are whole again
no Abu Bakr
no curfew
bobol is ting to laugh at again
because Black Stalin's voice is hoarse
but the North Stand is carrying him
Peter, keep de fire blazin'

and Pan in A Minor is a climax beneath us all
Jit is pastor preacher communion
and Renegades is choir
we   willing submittants to this cult
because Kitchener decided to explore
the minor chord

before Brooklyn before Temper before hurt
Beat Pan
before gang fight before poetry before debt
Beat Pan

before kidnappings before crack
Beat Pan
before reconciliation with my father

before this rapture and this bruise
before this longing to make it up to Trinidad
and have Trinidad apologize to me
before wear red and lose to America in football
before 9-11 before cut locks before these poems
before Bush threatened to cut off aid
we never wanted in the first place

it was always the Savannah
always the North Stand
always Kitch making the Pan sing
in chords it never knew it had in it
for Spree for Trinidad for the flag woman
for the pelau woman
for me and a Texan
in a hot kitchen
in Brooklyn

Melda's song

Nastiness goin cause your death
Gyul no man cyah stan yuh breath
You too damn nasty; get away from me

(Chorus) Melda, Oh yuh makin' weddin' plan
Carryin' meh name to obeah man
All you do; yuh cyah get through
I still eh go marrid to you…
      Mighty Sparrow (from *Obeah Wedding*, sometime in the 50s)

Wonder what you do this man
 to have your name carved
so ignominiously into the psyche
of a nation for posterity.
You, iconic bad woman
husbandless, desperate spinster
we should believe you
disgraced by aloneness, and so challenged
turned to the vagaries of sorcery
to secure station in society.

Your breath was really stink, Melda
or did you get the bad rake from
another man scorned in public?
Were you seeking supernatural retribution
of the night, or simply demanding
that a promise be kept as another
man spilled his seed inside you left you
to be the laughing stock of a narrow
fanged village wallowing in the muck
of its several incestuous layers of colonialism?

We know the old bard, Melda.
Could croon a song for a long time now
and Papa could tell a good story

16

but we also know his carousing ways
the women half his age left
in the wake of his famous promises,
and mysterious gap-toothed children
with an ear for a good tune.
Don't leave us the one-side story Melda.
Pick up a guitar or something.

Been thinking about you,
wondered what you looked like.
He spoke to you
whispered in your ear once
the Vat 19 like mud on his tongue
as he reached a hand down
to caress your ass.
A dark woman — simple
you happened by the rum shop
one evening as the man held court,
all his prize monies and calypso titles
sparkling out of that braggadocios laugh.
You wore a simple shift; sandals on your feet.
He was relatively young; you too
but not so young the whispers
hadn't already begun.
Zamie, Chupidee, she cyah make chile.
Your hair was separated into four
neatly combed sections; a thick plait
hanging richly from each — I know
you only pass there for some salt prune, Melda
but the man, as easily as he could sing a tune
could charm the wings off an angel; and he did.

He was a handsome one, that Slinger
in the days when he was still
making mischief — dodging white handled
razors on the Quay. He said

enough to get you to let him walk you
home that night. He came back
twice more, professing love and grand things.
You lay down with him outside — under the fig tree
not risking to wake your aunt and grandmother
with the creaking springs. Maybe, heady
moment it was; vision of his future
so attractive, you didn't mind the small
rooming house he took you to entering
you in a rush — like a man beaching
on a familiar island, eager to subdue the natives.

What happened the first time you asked
for him at the rum shop, Melda?
Rheumy-eyed old men all of a sudden
thought it alright to pass a stray hand
over your breast. Tired wives, gathered
round the stand pipe began the phlegmy rumors —
the rhythm section of the song that posterizes
you forever as ugly as whore or worse.
Did they, finally relieved that they were respectable,
that for once they hadn't to worry
about their men with this one, cooyah their mouths
as you passed by? None of them ever
thought you pretty (you were always too black)
but envied you your build; tall, long-legged,
broad-shouldered; they saw how their men
watched you. They envied your silence,
your reserve like a cloudy night.

What happened the first time you dared
ask him "What about me?" Did you
find out about the other woman
only five blocks away? Did you threaten

to tell her? Did he lie and dismiss you
or did he make a scene, right there
in the middle of the valley, right
by the rum shop where the taxis turn around?
He sent you home, rum taut on his breath
as the men cleared their throats. Could you
hear as you left, the bottle and spoon rhythm
in the distance as this newest calypso blossomed
into the ugly, evil spell it became?
At the end, you threatened the obeah man
just to deflect the shame as you turned
your back just in time that they shouldn't
see the bright shine growing in your eye,
or hear the first crash as the tear hit
the pavement with the weight of blood and forever
and shame and lifetimes of sex that was for them
but not for you — lifetimes of whores and saga boys
spoilt women and dashing, coveted men
ballads for good girls and raucous drinking songs
for the sluts who dared bring their black, ashy
faces down to the rum shop to claim
what was promised them.

You're still alive — have one child,
a boy, not by the bard. You moved from the valley
shortly after, but not before the man won the calypso
monarchy on your back and children sang it
in the unforgiving streets while pointing at you
and repeating words they heard in their parents'
drawing rooms long after they'd been sent to bed.
Thank God the boy, your son, never figured out
who that song was about. It was long off the
airwaves by the time he was old enough to understand,
and he was always too strapping and too serious;
too thoughtful and too polite for anyone to dare

tell him about this song about his mother;
you taught him well. But you have a story
and you cannot sing, and there is a truth
keeping you alive, keeping away the madness
when the night becomes still, when the night
is only the croaking of a restless crapaud and
the faint tinkle of a bottle and spoon in the distance.
Pick up a guitar or a shot glass — pull up
your rocking chair and your still proud frame,
Melda. Tell me the story. Sing me that song.

Dorothy coming down

Cause de Ku Klux Klan still in Alabama
And in Brixton, England,
my people still under pressure
anytime I see that South Africans are free
yes, ah goin an finish de whole damn calypso bout Dorothy…

…but while my people still fightin
With so many children's lives at stake
Wait Dorothy, wait Dorothy, wait…
                                    Black Stalin — *Dorothy (1985)*

The black dread begs Dorothy some time
to fix some things before she makes her appearance
traps her inside a sweet calypso
while he plays the messiah she must await

see Dorothy wait impatient
for the song that will make her
flesh blood memory

Dorothy waits in Laventille
and Flatbush Avenue always four children
and a one-room house in the background
for a miracle any miracle hand on hip
for some messiah to end a war
or fill a barrel to send back

waiting for a single carnival moment
a jam to end all exploitation
skirt a little too short waiting
cleavage corpulent and exposed
dress a little too tight — waiting
but who will do this work
this poor people's work

in Brixton in Alabama in South Africa
in Port-of-Spain in Brooklyn
Dorothy waiting

for a signal from this one dread
but frustration is a scar on Dorothy's shoulder
lights her pent-up fuse

Dorothy is a Molotov cocktail
waiting for a flag a horn a battle-cry
to explode into tune and color
Dorothy waits

after lovers and husbands have left
Dorothy waits
while politicians lie and get away
Dorothy waits
combs her children's hair and hopes
still waiting
powders her chest shines her face
and grabs her purse

wait Dorothy   wait Dorothy   wait…

Dorothy thunders off
prancing to a new six-bass
the song might be enough to call her
not enough to hold her back

Dorothy is coming down the hill
to fix the mess herself
this watching for messiahs is fockery
let someone else wait
Dorothy has work to do

Act Two

And you, my father,...
Curse, bless, me now with your fierce tears, I pray
Do not go gentle into that good night.
Rage, rage against the dying of the light

Dylan Thomas

what the water gave me

(after Frida Kahlo)

The water gave me madness
incessant humming blood

the water remembers the torn torso
melting through a seashell's portholes

the quadrangular tight-rope of death
disease slaughtered women the trade
in gold and spirit of five hundred nations drifting

the water remembers   the water is clarity
the water remembers   offers back hurricane
the water remembers hides its secrets

no wonder water remembers in tectonic shifts
and the angry expectorant of lava

no wonder water runs muddy revolts
to flood and brackish

no wonder water stays still in the dark
the water is coming back home

seahorses

Mother searches her dreams for fish
has given up hope
for the daughter-in-law
figures a grandchild is the most
she can ask

For the first time I want
to give her the daughter
she miscarried in my twelfth year
bring a child like sacrifice
to her altar — to her unfulfilled dreams for me

I have given her no other sacrifices
brought none of the tithings
she has asked for raising me
I want to give her the one she missed
whom she'd already named   Nyasha

Nothing is so frightening
as the spirit overcoming intent
I make love like an act
of revolution desperation dissent

Every square synapse of every woman
I touch feels like a savannah
of possibility and motherhood
Nyasha screams in my belly

every time   We drown her out
but lately she'll have none of it
She has teetered on the edge
of the guf waiting for years now

she is swimming closer
she'll beat up the boys
ignore my advice

My mother would be proud
the child will recognize her flesh
swim with fish in her own dreams
she will always have been wanted

unplanned / gift

find myself
    wanting this
an impractical
sentimental fool

bring you the news
like a paper-boy

brusque careless
mimicking masculinity

    your voice is mine
    deep soft laughter

even through the phone
        father
we are mirrors

in the same breath as my father

we come from a long line of dancers   African men
  fan gaudy plumage to attract lovers
  bristle feathers in cockfight aggression
even now we are the stickfighter's jumps and twirls
salvos of Bois! echoing in our pasts
save all these for the passage of manhood rites

today you and I circle each other with politician guile
make tentative offerings as men will
skirt our emotions deftly
dress them in bravado   and control

I hear my own laugh come back
and the circle is broken
more and more they say I am becoming your image
wonder if I can keep up
your devotion to progressiveness
remind myself I too sacrifice many things
for an understanding many will call   frivolous

when we deign to speak
I offer forgiveness
   immediately bile in my throat
like the bitter guilt of giving away something
not belonging to you
to someone who does not need it

I have no other questions for you Father
all the answers are coming to me on the corridors of time
my failures and in stark moments of clarity

someone who has never met you
said of me recently:
beware of him; he is just like his father

Just now I know I will wear that mantle like ribbon
  that I would spit their comments back at them like bullets
if I were worthy enough to shoot on your behalf
if as my shoulders square into yours
and my chest expands to mimic you
I could build a life of work and struggle
mentionable in the same breath as my father

pretender to a throne
I am still filling out the mandate of your life

they will say of you you know
here is nothing but an old man
trying to make amends for youthful wrongs…
they will say:
here is the child; bearing magnanimous exoneration…
they will not have met you
or know how much I still must learn
in order to have that right
how many more dances must be completed
for the passage of these rites

I am only precocious
blighted label of potential badged
on my sternum like a leper's bell
only talking   only becoming
not yet realized
and foolishly I have spoken out of turn

please forgive me my father
please forgive me my father
I have become you   inadequately

photo graph

the focus might be the bougainvillea
  behind the two men the flowers brag
a flourish of burgundy

their shirts
less clothing   more plumage
orange rust white
they are grinning together
  the first time in their lives (it seems)
  twenty-four years and the fear of irrelevance
separate them
make them kin

father finally comfortable
boy finally accepting

turn the photo around
watch what blooms

Bullet Points
— *Hyacinth Bonair's 1974 manifesto on race*

1.
You are Black. Not Negro
Not Nigger
Not Brown. Not Mixed
Not you have some German on your mother's side from your great-
grandfather because no-one can see that anyway
You are Black
(dis is how yuh dance to calypso)

2.
Be proud of being Black
of course your hair is wooly
because you're black
and it's beautiful
that's why it's in an Afro
Don't let anyone cut your hair again
as long as I'm around

3.
Your father called
He said "Happy Birthday"

4.
White people cannot be trusted
Be cordial. Be polite
but white people must prove themselves
before they can be trusted

5.
Don't ever bring a white woman to this house
whom you would not bring if she were black
e.g., if you wouldn't date a black waitress
don't parade a white one in here

6.
In fact
Don't bring a white woman in this house

7.
Marilyn Monroe is not a loose woman
She has the right to make love
to whomever she chooses
(dis is how yuh jump to calypso when yuh crossin'
the savannah stage)

8.
Do not bring
a white woman in this house

9.
Indira Gandhi is the most important black woman in the world
(dis is how yuh chip to calypso late Tuesday evenin' when yuh tired)

10.
Indian people are black people too
it's just that most of them don't know it

11.
This book is by Linton Kwesi Johnson. Read it.
This book is by Sonia Sanchez. Read it.
This book is by Walter Rodney. Read it.
This book is by Charles Dickens. Read it.
This book is by Enid Blyton. Read it.
This poem is by Kamau Braithwaite. memorize it
and return in an hour

12.
A is for Africa
B is for Black
C is for culture
and that's where it's at
(dis is how yuh fete hard durin' last lap when yuh ketch
yuh second wind)

13.
Your father called
he sent these things
He said "Merry Christmas"
(dis is how yuh get up Ash Wednesday morning and go to school no matter
how much rum yuh drink Carnival Tuesday)

your father called...

armed into the night

I am living the language of my mother, culling words off her tongue,
cramped inside her closed vowels, breaking out only to curse the lan-
guage boxing me and freeing me, her words spelling our names into
legacy.

no fathers there, only deeds for descendants to recount, deeds living
in a vortex of language, of words with which to inflect the silences we
inherit; our black silence and woman silence and family silence and
father silence; and all around us the silence at least three generations
deep, so we can't know where it was first born, though we know when
we thought first to kill it, thought to free it to innuendo, to give it shape
and color, to abandon it to the well and call it back up baptized.

A haughty English and rhythmic dialect strung together on the stout
cord of understanding; words, epiphanies, interrogatives filling the single
turned instant between the flipping of the domino and the crash on a
flimsy table, tinkle of an ice cube and the gulp of scotch before laughter
— the cord, the only thing holding us in times all our staccato colorings
eons apart and growing farther, when the steep fluency of her language
is a hill I will not climb, when my words head out armed into the night —

she will not follow.

Waiting for Carla

when it's noon and the cellphone
pressed to your ear
feels like a brand
   cars roll by in slow motion
   birds flap their wings languidly
   become one in speed with clouds

when you're waiting for an answer
when Carla from St. Louis on the other end
has become a conspirator

when *Genetic Technologies* feels like the hand of God
delivering you from a future of pressures
someone else would have you take

you cannot cry
you cannot think
about the infant's dark pupils
following the sound of your voice

you must not remember
his newborn grip on your finger
his smile just last week

you must forget the wanting
to see him crawl
the hoping he might some day
write stories kick a ball be proud of his father

you must let go all of these

wait for the tinny reality of Carla's voice
what is your case number
what is the password
is this for a paternity test

      think about the truth
      how much he will need
      to be proud of his father
      how hard that will be
      if he will never see you kiss
      his mother. How much easier
      the truth will be
      than the negotiation of weekend visits
      diaper changes PTA meetings
      first time he turns an ankle

when you're waiting for the answer
and the tarmac ahead looks like forever
and your friend is waiting
beside you to hold your hand or high-five you

when the words you tend like garden
desert you and all you can hear
is your heart beating
the echo of your own father's voice
the wailing of your mother's

forget how he kicked in your lap
how he nestled in your arms
do not think about wiping his tears

Act Three

And the women will find him and wrap him in silks
and the women will teach him and bathe him in oils
and the women will dress him for battle and for love
and the women will call him back home

Lay me Down

Venus Asleep (Oil on Canvas) b. Paul Delvaux

Praise the night and its watchful eyes
the bones marking time in the corner of the room

Praise Jah and the bronzing moon
coveting our coupling bodies

Praise the erotic touch building us
from floor to air pillar to mountain

Praise this bush that marks me
this bed that lays me down

Praise these women in their finery
their menses like covenant

Praise these bones these beckoning feet
these breasts this vulva

Praise the floor that reminds me
I am tree and water and earth and crossing

Praise the mountains and the heavens
the armies and their queens

Praise this waking and the color
voice of painter and of poet

Praise the dream of arms and torsos
lips and devious tongues

Praise the hip-bone and the rising belly
the supple bodies of my lovers

who lay me down
who lay me down

To Kali

*"…a hymn to the goddess (Kali) describes her as dancing wildly and
making the world shake."*   David Kinsley

For certain I am not nearly ready
for the tiny eruption of toes and fingers
 your warrior howls

you will be dark and multi-tiered
 woman and complex
already I know your hands
on your stout hips
defiant sare at your father

we will make each other weep
because you will try to take over the world
I will wear my mother's cloak
    try to tame you

your kinetic energy is already moving
inanimate objects uprooted in shock from
their moldings — likely I will do something
banal — find a job — start a trust fund
talk to you in-utero
the failing of all egotistical male gods
creation in my own image and likeness

defy me refuse my feeble genes
throw off the constricting cloak
map stars and moons instead of cities
learn and question and doubt
believe and create and challenge
refuse to write poems
 sculpt goddesses instead
refuse my sports

possible my dreams for you are just that —
dreams   you will crush with your
several sworded arms to replace
with your own vision

and I will laugh at your defiance
  love your scowl
scream my own screams against it

carve mold burn this earth
as you see fit

but whatever you do make it new
make it whole create it in your image
woman   dance wildly; make the world shake

phantom limbs

Everything now is the light
receding from the light
till alone is the only thing
that calls from this dark town.
trying not to cry (or panic)
convince myself this is just
astigmatism
the pain; temporary withdrawal symptom

*

This week, all my friends have babies. They love me. "Do it again; do it again, Uncle Rog!" The bills are paid. I move with the easiness of a man satisfied to have seen the sliver of light. I have spoken to both my fathers today. They are happy, things are steady these days. They worry, I am already them, their time to get it right; done — their legacies, in my hands.

*

call my mother.
catch a movie. work. pay more bills
someone asks about you
your spot on my bed aches
like a phantom limb

*

you think this is easy?
the staying; running away
negotiating the safety net of this town
jumping for the safety net of you?
some days   I'm getting closer to getting it right
some nights — only the crying
rubbing the empty spots to warmth
itching phantom limbs to life

blue sex prodigy

I am blue sex prodigy
  so if you feel me at your feet
and in your mouth simultaneously
I am not God   only talented

surreal tongues of aura drawing strength
  from the moon's throat
your womb is only my way there
  and I refuse to make love to your womb
my sex comes only in shades of blue
          and night is blue   and indigo is blue
    and sky is blue   and sea is blue and you
are fertile with lust the vessel   my compass to immortality
you and me are three are sex in simulcast multiplicity
listen to the moans around us

my seventh tongue will claim you
concubine and bed you in poetry
innocence and savoir-faire
within me
  the product of Sun-Ra's last orgy
child of the moon
three planets
the sun
born in Taurus
the reason bulls run

listen to them running
listen to them coming
listen to them running
taurus bulls are coming
Pamplona opens her legs and her fingers start strumming
  and explodes in a festival
        my seventh tongue humming

Gluttony and Envy
Greed Wrath Sloth and Pride

all met their demise one kiss and they died
six mortal sinners all ground to the dust
only one living   and I am that lust
                                   I am that lust!

children born of orgies breathe metaphors
and suckle on the breasts of innuendo
images imprint ink on their irises
and they in turn spawn pages and pages of prophecy
I cannot stop this   and I cannot be yours alone
          there I slip again into your mouth
          down your throat and around your rhythm
          not God, but we splattered on incense
          wild twisted and free
I am growing by the moment
my seventh tongue has claimed you   claimed we

sex you and you altogether
fuck you for strength and drink of you for pleasure
lock up your daughters and sedate your wives
  blue is the color   of the joy of our lives
and I am blue man
living on blue planet
swimming in blue sea
eating blue food
I am Taurean lust
blue is we

so if you feel me at your throat
  and your womb's sex is full
  all over you wet trampled by bulls
naked and charged with the glow of sex light
examine your colors and the lust of your night
my suck on your flesh   your thick lips on me
trembling awaiting
blue sex prodigy

America: 1878 - called

1.
I do not come when called
Mostly I materialize

Dark as a kiss
incarnate again
  and again
sometimes twice in one life
now mother
 now the burnt sugar sweet
of a wide-eyed wide-hipped
too-young lover

now concubine
now priest

I do not come
I am called
when the wayward rib
needs me

2.
America is a dark continent
1878   exploding
industrializing
all over   my black behind

When I am called
I arrive   black bitch
whore   hard-ass
when I am called
 I run   fugitive
slave-codes   Reconstruction
I've incarnated into the open
rotted mouths of my own lovers

just to know   like they know
burnt
swinging

3.
I dance in the clearing
I laugh too loud
I give benediction
I show off my knickers
   and smell like funk
   like ragtime
   like fiddle and bucket-bass
I walk the long road North
I come when called
I ghost
I materialize
I moan
I dark continent
         sweating
I incarnate
   then come

I high lace collar
   pretending
I don't shuck and jive
I survive
I nigger   I black
I fuck massa in the barn
I serve tea in the big house
I collect Oscar and whipped back
I exposed super-bowl nipple
I Hottentot
I dark continent

4.
don't tell me 'bout Africa
no more

Amos and Andy are coming
Toni Morrison is coming
Michael Jackson and Tito Puente are coming
Tuskegee and Kent State are coming
Muhammad Ali is coming
Clarence Thomas and Condoleezza

I incarnate I birth pain
I know the bird
of my next life
          singing
coming
    called
                    mother
  concubine
  songbird
              priest
fuck for love
for power
tomorrow
          I traitor   conscience
          fading
                come

Act Four

"Fly like a butterfly / sting like a bee
your hands can't hit / what your eyes can't see
Rumble young man, rumble…"
Bundini Brown on Muhammad Ali

we come far

one foot in the calabash; forging a path to a new era
        Brown University Caribbean Week Convocation — 2004

Haiti I'm sorry, we misunderstood you
Some day we'll turn our heads
And recognize you
        David Rudder — *Haiti*

and still coming
  still coming
we still filling up planes
making our way north
past Independence   past self-government
past the first generation of aging ailing Rasta
to chant down / chant for / chant in spite of Babylon

and from every island
in every tongue we hold onto
whatever fiction we need
to call ourselves home — wave flags import music
we put a carnival jump-up in any city
still not terrorist (or nigger) phobic enough
to allow the immigrant darkies
space to congregate as long as we
could blame some violence on them afterwards
so we hold on

one foot forever in the calabash
say we forging a path to a new era
we come here year after year
wearing these old colonies on our sleeves
these old lies on our tongues
we better than them black Americans
we could make it here
dem yankee an dem too lazy
while we work domestic for white folk
who swear on their liberal democratic vote

for another not-so-republican-republican
so their mutual funds don't suffer
while they pat the sweet interesting
Haitian Antiguan Jamaican Trinidadian maid
on her $300 a week and no health insurance head

all this so we could send a barrel back
to assuage our guilt
one foot in the calabash the other covered
in Nike Phat Farm Timberland Levis Gap
but we making progress
last month able to send home enough money
to put a new roof on Mama house
to make sure the boy can take
extra lessons for Common Entrance

We movin' outta Brooklyn jes now
not livin' amongst dem yankee niggas no more
we goin' Jersey where we could have a backyard
one more year and I can apply for citizenship
ah could work over the table go to school now
leave de asshole man ah had to marrid
fuh de green card

In Trinidad we try to understand
what with the fashion of kidnappings
and gang land rubouts
Dale was shot 14 times two weeks ago
and I wish I had spoken with him
since we left primary school
the crack finally killed Selwyn's son
but we almost up from under
the already-done-its-damage IMF
so we calling in Giuliani to tell us
to tell black folk what to do about crime
one foot stuck in a calabash…

Haiti I'm sorry
We misunderstood you…
America is still punishing Haiti
for the audacity of the Black Jacobin revolution
forging always a new poverty
through its rank and file Disney-sweatshopped reality
but the children are here
they're doing well
Yves did a brilliant book report
on Columbus yesterday for school
and his teachers say on his report card
He's a natural athlete. You should get him into basketball camp
while the Jamaican dollar hits 60 to 1
so they can support Hanes and whomever else
in the Free Trade sectors
so we can ensure with our dollars here
that we'll only ever elect
a conservative capitalist there

trying to forge paths to new eras 25 years now
but Grenada still stinks to us
newly colonized by United We Stand These Colors don't Run
and we'll invade your country and destabilize it
if you try to make your people conscious
stick yourself back in your calabash
or we'll withdraw your aid
and while you're at it
we want immunity from prosecution
in your international courts
and your best beachfront properties
Amen there are more evangelist tents
than ever dotting our countrysides
reminding us that if we sit tight
God will give us our due
just don't bother registering to vote

when you get here
because if your last name is French
you're black
and living in Florida
then that one-foot calabash
might be your turn-the-clock-back
to 1954 Mississippi grave and…

Haiti I'm sorry…
we're making progress
hear the steel pan on Eastern Parkway
Heather Headley on Broadway
Samuel Dalembert in the NBA
Aristide somewhere in Africa
Colin Powell in the White House

send back a barrel
with a journal of our histories
so we can remind ourselves
in the new order of things
what we did to make such progress
who we sacrificed
to come this far

The future of America in the belly of the beast
(the millennium edition)

I am going back
to the overtly political poem

one in which black men still
are called animal
on the front page of newspapers

in which Donald Trump
takes out a full-page ad
calling for the death penalty for five teens

and 13 years later carries no story
when DNA evidence exonerates them

for now, I eschew the complex symbolism
of history and family and love
and art as revolution

today I'm just telling it like it ain't
naked   simple   stark
              They are still...

as arrogant as a president
who says 'fuck you' to the rest of the world
"i'll wage war when I damn well please"

as obvious as: Al Qaeda is the product
of the Pakistani secret service
which is sponsored by the CIA

as blatant as glaring
as all the companies that sold all their stock
on September 10, 2001

today, I cannot justify
 the erotic poem — the living
of sexual freedom as transcending
existing social boundaries

because they took Mumia
off Death Row and knew we'd forget
he is still locked up

and they're trying to tell us
that Biggie killed Tupac
while the LAPD ignores all the evidence in Biggie's murder

today fuck craft form
can kiss my natural black ass
can only say it how I see it
the Central Park jogger cannot pursue
new evidence in her rape
because the statute of limitations is up and fucked up

and she was beat so bad
she can't remember the details
                    ...*still killing the buffalo*

and hormone injected meat
and DNA manipulated vegetables
with two months shelf life are
forced down our throats

and Latin American governments manipulated
to clear the way for US multi-nationals
    must get overt here   call names
back to the guileless political poem

Dole Fruit   Chiquita Banana
                     They are still killing the buffalo

and the man who managed to steal
two elections in the world's greatest democrazy
 now wants a national ID card system

no time for metaphor or clever
US supported the South African apartheid regime
in the fight against black folk in Angola

and we can't figure out
why someone would want to fly a plane
into so many gleaming stacks of currency
                              ...still

        see the buffalo dwindle on the plains
        see women and children die at Wounded Knee
        see Mexicans broken in the fields
        see Reconstruction deconstructed
        again and again and again

see single mothers, wailing sisters
and angry wives
all gather in front the downtown Brooklyn jails
        the LA county jails
        the Newark city jails
        still killing

see Guiliani's cops execute another
on Church Avenue
on Beverly Street
in Washington Heights
in Hell's Kitchen

no time for metaphor   no time for symbol
I'm returning to the original   overt   guileless   political poem

They are still killing the buffalo
They are still killing the buffalo
They are still killing the buffalo

song for Trent Lott
(who said we'd be a better country today if
Strom Thurman had won the presidency)

You think you'd have survived
that vote Mr. White Man
do you know what we do in the dark?

we took your rags and made rope
took your kindling and grew fruit
picked your cotton and crafted reconstruction
that slave-barrack hunger rages in our history

this too we take into the dark

take it with our dances and our languages
huddle close to it
in the Georgia cold or Alabama cold or Maryland cold

who we be?
you can't know us
we surviving the crossing and the crossings

we making it onto auction block
and first-round draft pick
we crossing ocean and swamp
we descendants of amputees and unknown fathers
ridges with welts and patience

all this we take into the dark
at night where you will not follow
where you'd rather cut your losses on a nigger
than lose two more bloodhounds to the chase

we have survived

imagine what we hold
in the corners in our shadows

who survive Tuskegee and small-pox blanket
heroin and Cointelpro
project housing and Jim Crow
Lynchburg VA and Lynchburg PA
Lynchburg TX
and the whole muthafuckin' state of Mississippi

we feed on that slave barrack dust
grow fat on your hatred
bleed songs and tap-dances
from your left-overs
imagine who we be
the sardine shipment
rapes
beatings
castrations
humiliation

what son of Denmark Vesey you wanna fuck wit?
what child of Tubman or Assata you wanna run wit?
what son of Cuffy L'Ouverture or Douglass?
what Nat Turner progeny is in our dark corners
waiting to rise?
seed of Huey child of Malcolm Amistad badass
you think you wanna follow into this absurd future
not knowing the difference between backs and walls?
what child of Crazy Horse you think you wanna fight?

these too we take into the dark
into these mysterious folds of skin
under arms and between our legs
backs of our throats
and all them swamps you don't wanna follow through
East New York, Brooklyn and Oakland, California
Fifth Ward, Houston and South Side, Chicago

every reservation every store-front church
every Erzulie ritual and Santero offering
what buffalo soldier you think you want
turnin' on yo ass?

what hip-hop beat or gospel growl you want
raising spirits against you?
what zydeco what capoeira you want
holding a gun to your head?
we who survive Ku Klux Klan and Move bombings
who didn't get thrown overboard
who didn't get sick in the passage

this shit ain't no coincidence
all this we take into the dark
grow stink to fester like culture

you don't want none of this Mau Mau shit
none of this Panther shit
this Black Jacobin shit
from we who survive
Giuliani and Jasper, Texas

you think this shit would have been easier?

Bird Watching

(after Martín Espada)

Manolo sees the birds first
 "los pajaros, los pajaros!"
he always sees them first
is a dreaming man
"I have plans outside these alcachofas" he always says
so he's watching the sky

good thing about California
the birds will always signal
the renegade crop-duster
 drunk   snarling pilot can't always wait
for the stinking Mexican cockroaches
to get out   before he showers pesticide
 hellish rain
from a low-flying demon-engine

most days drunk and angry
he can never drink enough to wash the olive hue
of his Mexican mother off his skin
can never drink enough to forget
the mother he never knew
or the taunts of the children
his white father raised him around
la cucaracha, la cucaracha…

 so now he revs the engine
 making gauntlet of the little brown cockroaches

most days they get to the huts just in time
except for that once that Jaime
looked up for too long
one side of his face still has the burn discoloration
one eye   still blind and cloudy

the pickers scatter   some sacks and tools
gathered up by instinct

others dropped in panic
women keep pace with their husbands   brothers   sons

the sound of the plane will scare
flocks of white egret up early enough
that if you see the sudden panicked flight
you have at least thirty seconds to get to the huts unharmed
   nature has already selected for industry

as one shroud the birds undulate into the air
bank left out of the path
of the thing with bigger wings
and drift a light scarf toward the hills

Manolo is in full stride
by the time he finishes his plea
negrito face almost flushed with fear and heat
   Jaime is picking up pace too
 the memory of searing pain twitching in his one good eye

all moving now as one
a flock of brown birds scampering for their nest
broken wings unable to bank out of the way

but one small boy is falling
twelve years old   it is his first day in the field
his father Palacio, a serious, practical man
pulled him out of class that day
   tienes que apprender como hacer eso…
 - you have to learn how to do this…
you might as well — he had told him

Palacio never looks up from his work
and the boy mimics him — wants to get this right

even though he would have preferred
to be in school today

they're learning quadratic equations
and he is excited because he has already figured it out
his English is poor so he is more interested
in the world of symbols and numbers and pictures
but he wants to make Papa proud too

Palacio screaming   reaches
a frantic hand back for his son
but they are flagging dangerously now
and the tequilad pilot is laughing at the sport of it
two slow Mexican cockroaches
caught out with the lights on
la cucaracha, la cucaracha!!

Manolo refuses to be a picker anymore
spends his time finger-picking sad cantos
on his guitar — enamel cup catching with a dull clatter
the drizzle of coins that will keep him in tequila
as workers go in and out of the cantinas

rancheros pass by and sneer at him
  lazy dog... as they toss coins at his head
  si, pero tambien la lluvia no me va alcanzar
the rain won't catch me though —

Palacio is a sky-watcher now — a dreamer
none of his other children will come to the fields
since his boy's arms and chest burned
and he screamed for three days
  but Palacio has daughters
so he's always looking at the sky *los pajaros, los pajaros*

first thoughts of a come-again messiah when informed of the protocol of the new crucifixions *(for Man-man)*

Begin me as you always have
  with the whip
base idolater of your fields and cities
Understand nothing of the hell you promise
the agony   crowns of thorns and such

but you are a man
so know this
your son if he were born soon
and Black would be the wellspring
of your tears —
the woman by whom you made him
nothing but a historically discarded Magdalene
          Look up her name
  see how many embittered sons of Cain
you raise together
how much parched earth you till

Your son if he were born soon
and Black would author the first
of our original thoughts
the only dialogue you'd ever hear
or he fears the only dialogue
you'd have the will to permit
filled with guns and beatings
raped women and fierce outlandish dreams
you would scream   to see the scars
keloided into mountains for him to cross
through snarl and desert
and beseech   "Father Father why hast
thou forsaken me?"

Begin him again me again
your son born of your soil

lately and Black with lash and salt for supper
with murdered tongue and Magdalene woman
trembling on a dirt floor
beneath cross and thorns and scars
thoughts of flight or massacre
when he might have been begun
of clan and extended family
of matriarch and laughter
of sweat and gift exchange

Would you teach him again
the layered music of hate
or let this woefully insufficient time
cradle him for breast-milk and healing
would you rock this boy your son
turned out of door one thousand times before

Would you swaddle him
Or say again
          "the king needs enemies and wars
              the people; messiahs and foils for uprising?"

Say you would begin him again
  me again
 would you choose again
for your own son
new and separate crucifixion
turn his friends against him
with promises of land silver and renown
deliver him again
despite the efforts
of his Peters his Pauls his Sitting Bulls
his Robesons ambassadors and Malcolms?

deliver him again to priests and smart bombs
gated suburbs and religions
dissatisfied with their own truths?

to infested blankets and destabilization
World Bank and sweatshop labor
suffer the children to rip at each other's throats
rather than come unto socialism?

deny him his brother's love
even if it could gift him
nights under the stars and smell of juniper?

If you could bring us milk and grass and sunlight
would you offer us again dog and hose
and nothing but a discourse with death?

Your son born soon and Black
will know gun wound and sacrifice
will call you to precincts and court houses

Time is neither accurate nor enough
but begin him again, and softly
see everything you touch
shed its scars like a dead seasons past skin
see it all fade soon   to Black

Truth applies for a green card

Truth say that if he could get a cheap flight
someone to sponsor him
a newspaper a TV station
anything to give him some play
he'd move out
bring a sacred cow or two with him
ride through the streets
with laurels round his neck

but Truth say he's got HIV and arthritis diabetes
Truth say he applied for green card
but ain't nothin' movin'
nobody wants to bring Truth to America Truth say
so Truth stay in India
losing weight
cuz not the Brahmins or the Buddhists
the Untouchables or the government
wants to feed him

the missionaries offer Truth some food
if he'd come to Christ
but Truth say Truth can't do that
Truth is truth   after all

and say ain't no god with no white beard
in no heaven
ever gonna be bigger than him

For John Hollander

so many of us crowd the subway
almost all dark tired on the way to work
including the smiling homeless man
who reeks so that he has an entire three-seater to himself
and the beautiful young woman in the corner stealing glances at her
reflection in the window

above us as part of the Poetry in Motion series Hollander's poem
blesses our putrid lives with art
his piece there — something about a sheet of paper with a heart cut
out of the middle

meadows of hopefulness he muses from on high
empty or open-hearted? he asks of his surly wards
I am reading this sterling work
from a great contributor
over and over again trying to glean reason from *'meadows'*
and *'fair spring days'*

I have been crying over love
these past two days
would be willing to hold on to any fantasy of truth

but the people around me look tired and poor
the homeless man is chuckling to himself
the woman in the corner is stealing glances at my confusion

world going by station by station   unimpressed

Act Five

"When the lights go down in the city
and the sun shines on the bay
I want to be there in my city…"

Journey (*Lights*)

Spring
(after e. e. cummings)

 and the balls dance
out on the asphalt courts

baggy shorts oversized white tees
  and JamaalandTyrone
swagger in
and the chains
       swish
trash talk and more bouncing echoes

and the blueandwhite cruiser   comes by slowly

Spring
  and the girls fix their hair
corn rows to afro puffs
spring
and short jeans skirts
white tennis
spring
and YvetteandTasha walk slowly
by the ricochet of
  bouncing balls
  boys taking it to the hole
and the blueandwhite cruiser
sirens once
                 twice

Spring

and the boys freeze
slow their games
  smooth guile of a stroll
spring and 5-O
flashes lights again

and EddieandKahil watch
from inside the chain-link court

Spring and
  dogwood blossoms
 dust the green-painted asphalt
and fifty boys bolt
in fifty directions

and 5-O chooses
a pair of fifteen-year olds
to chase
spring and their guns are drawn
spring and the flat report
  rings into the Sunday afternoon
of a store-front church
  swing-low
sweet chariots coming
and their lights are flashing
  and there are mothers wailing
    the makeshift altars' flowers
    on the hot asphalt court will
fade by summer
spring
  and a ball rolls slowly to the street
  and somewhere in the city
there is a quick siren
and boys running everywhere

how the ghetto loves us back

five-eleven in stilettos
and one hundred and eighty lbs

she wears yellow and royal blue
spandex down one leg
on the other   a batty-rider
cut-off fleshy ass exposed
at its lowest corner
and rounding into excellence

  this is how the ghetto loves us back

the matching top is a bikini
everything else falls into place
nose-ring attitude gum-popping
lips and nostrils flared
blue and yellow painted toenails
to remind us
this is no accident

women turn young children's faces
into their ugly pastel skirts
lift their carefully coiffed heads
and sniff the air for judgment
older men shake their heads
in public disapproval or to hide
the beginnings of their own erections

young girls look on in awe
equal parts amazement envy and
I want to be like her when I grow up
at the obvious mystic power
of the high jiggling ass
  the atmosphere is of festive ridicule

the most honest among us
the jobless and the laborers
hoot and holler from stoops and corners
shout at one another through windows
high above the streets
utter general and public
                    Goddamn(s)!
she ignores them all
except to once stop
fix her hair
 while exaggeratedly cocking the generous hips
to one side

none of us able to get
what we think is her stench
off our hands
can't cast our gazes away from her
as the scent grows stronger
rather than subsides
this ghetto scent
accentuated in the noonday heat
sweating up our palms
no less her pimps and molesters
no less her rapists
than whatever scarred the black back
of the exposed left thigh
than whatever strewed the crack vials
crunching under her heels
than whatever convinces her
to readjust the halter every 30 seconds

she fades into the bright white distance
and into our imaginations
past the grade-schoolers
jumping rope and cussing

in front of the Shiloh Baptist Church of the Redeemer
past the corner where Shaqwan's 13 year old blood
muddied up the sidewalk
past the four hair-dressing salons
the three take-out Chinese food restaurants
the two liquor-stores jeweled
  with bullet-proof glass

and the stench is still with us
a nuclear mushroom-cloud
but this is just how the neighborhood smells

like gun metal and acid
and struggle
and gym shoes and struggle
and crabs in a barrel   and struggle
and police cars
and little girls aspiring to video hair-dos
and struggle
and gentrification   and struggle
and the armpits of the second racist mayor in a row
and struggle
and struggle
and struggle
and struggle
and
  this is how it smells
now that we know
how much we don't love the ghetto
this is how it smells   how it feels
how it tastes
this is how the ghetto
loves us back

everything comes together — saga of a ghetto neighborhood

      yesterday the sun set
and all across the sky behind the bridge
was red
     black clouds rose up
  covered the sky —   mountains
changed from their familiar heavy savannah
to immediate ink

     The lights at the base of the bridge
 continued to look like two ships
side by side
    long after I knew they were the lights
at the base of the bridge
          — *todo que pasa combiene* —

   When night comes in Washington Heights
it does not arrive sudden or spectacular
 as it does in midtown
 It steals across the river
  through the bridge's girders
        With great anticipation,
 its secrets and traumas come
to the already beleaguered residents.

     — night in Washington Heights
can spell magic
  it is a festive thing
one huge gyrating ballroom —
 a mass of tie-dyed possibilities
plaintive ballads of lost love and
 remembered homes

80

Santo Domingo
Puerto Rico
Trinidad & Tobago

      maracas, merengue y la aroma
del carne guisada
    mix with crack whores
stale urine
and the gaze of racist cops.
      a mean and narrow reality
   infects men's hopes
 and when sky goes all red
behind the bridge
    the girders' shadows weigh
      heavier than yuppie gentrification
en el barrio
    poisonous malt liquor
leaps   a collective vulture
     off bodega shelves
         orange juice and ambition go stale
and all prisoners need comfort anyway
       — *todo que pasa combiene* —

— a man tilted all the way over
under the relentless pressure of a drug habit
and its methadone handmaiden
keeps our heavy humid breaths up
     sometimes
— he reminds blunt smokers
what they might become
  others,
      what they must struggle to avoid

His father was a junkie
          his father's father
— a virtuoso mariachi before the liquor
and arthritis took it away
          some debate which demon came first —
and this man, still sagging
   lost a battle in the womb
in the Heights — that most do not fight
'til adulthood
                    he never sang — he never held
his grandfather's storied guitar

          Night in the Heights
accommodates only the intrepid
but still offers the softness sometimes
of promise -
          — a teenage mother on her way to City College
          — jazz at St. Nich's bar
          — a soft jumper falling through a hoop
 a still-dreaming boy's college scholarship riding the ball's rotations

at the courts on 150th

          I spilled something red and sticky
on my shirt   last night
     and a woman   more beautiful
than the mountain's deep savannah
   older   wiser than the bridge's girders
laughs at me
          — *Papi, tienes esposa?* —
          — *no?* —
          — *let me wash that for you and make sure you eat tonight...* —
Lisa, from the Bronx, told me one night
 que   todo que pasa combiene

and in a life that had
visited a woman with only harsh mysteries
and poverty's bitter medicine
　　there was room to offer a slice
　of her warmth to a compadre

　　　　　and there is no way
　　　　to value the real estate of a town
　　　that takes angst and pain
　and kneads it back into love
for its tenants' flagging spirits

　　　　　darkness steals under the bridge
　　　　　through the 155th street graveyard
　　　　　burrows into steam pipes
　　　beneath the streets of Washington Heights
Ramon Hector y Luis play
dominoes and drink
　mamajuan
while telling tales of the junkie's mariachi grandfather
　　today　they decide
the liquor caused the arthritis
　... y todo que pasa combiene

everything comes together　again.

yesterday the sun set
all across the sky behind the bridge

"dey sen de boy America to study lawyer
is som kinda perform de boy say he performin'"

"Um-hmmm"

"…and he was a bright boy yuh know."

"Um-hmm"

"Go quite America an' waste he mudder good time and money"

"Um-hmm"

"Tun rasta mark up all he skin wid tattoo an all kinda bizness…"

"Um-hmm"

"de grandmudder mus be tunnin' in she grave"

"um-hmm buh de boy look strong doh, an he look happy
 doh worry wid dat. de boy doin alright fuh he self…"

naming and other Christian things

At 31, I learn that Lena is short for Magdalene
  one of those enigmas of biblical lore
whore found religion
I have often questioned her motives — this love of Jesus Christ
  this holy supplication to the son of Man

and I think about Lena my grandmother
  great big woman — skin of ashy obsidian
hair whitened by the burden of conviction
and I wonder about this business of weeping and foot washing;
        but I can only remember her iron hand and rigid schedules
  her admonition on catching me daydreaming on the outhouse roof
        — *Get down off that thing boy*
        — *You have your book to study*
        — *What kind of man do you intend to become?!*

I recall her jacking up of my equally stern grandfather
informing him of the folly
of any repeated attempts to hit her
        Never does Mary Magdalene come to mind
  not in the helpless 'weeping for the crucified' way
  not in the convenient Catholic depictions
of feminine frailty of morals and spirit
        I know of a Magdalene with fight
more Joan of Arc than Maid Marian
more Sojourner Truth than damsel in distress
  and I want to tell the withering two-dimensional ghost
  couched and crumpled at the foot of the cross
        — *Get up and fight woman!*
        — *Wake up and live if you love him!*
        — *Jack up the Pontius Pilate and refuse surrender*

At 3, I was beaten for disrespect of my grandfather
at 8, because I was satisfied with only a 75 in Math

because she knew   having fought battles based purely on conviction
that she was preparing a man for the holiest of crucifixions
      there would be no washing of feet here
      no flimsy eruption of tears
only the austerity of a warrior
and a Puritan insistence on perfection and effort
  the creases through her aged jowls softening
only when she thought I needed to eat   to get strong
        — Son yuh lookin thin; come and get some food

Naming orients one to his universe the Lakotas believed
a change in name meant a chance for improvement
for the child who was not doing well
        so having learned the root of my grandmother's name
I cannot summon the sympathy for Mary Magdalene
  cannot help her weep tears of distress
only wish I could retroactive a name change for her
show her my grandmother carrying 30 pound sacks of coffee
  dragging her swollen leg behind her
rising from her deathbed to fight her daughter's battles

One day if I am worthy of her expectations
I will become a man worth crucifying
and all her beatings
her lessons
her Puritanism and super-human strength
will have taught me
that surrender is not an option

On that day I expect to see
standing at the foot of whatever urban cross they fashion
all five-foot-ten of Lena
pointing one huge gnarled finger at me
  the shining authority of her eyes

coming from the black forest of her flesh
the white electricity of her hair
lips trembling in rage
      — *Get down off that thing boy and fight!*
      — *What kind of man do you intend to become?*

The sadness of migration
(after Barbara Ras)

is when you realize you've finally spent
more years in your adopted country
than you've lived in your own And the click
of that turnover makes you wonder
while you ride a crowded underground
train with children who sell chocolates
for non-existent basketball teams
whether this means the chalkboard
of equations of all the things
that make you you is slowly coming
erased If maybe the first time
you finally carved a crude cone
out of a wedge of pine
drove a nail through the center
and wound twine around its crooked spine
to make a top never really happened
If the trill of a home made kite on the wind
razor blade zwill searching the tails of
the other pretty birds in the air
would waft itself completely out
of the memory of all the things you held dear

One day you're a citizen of something small
but yours altogether and the hot asphalt
that binds you there the accent the jostling
taxis signaling for their chance at full meals
for their children the music and colorful costumes
the street corner ciphers mimicking
the air of something foreign your mother's calling
through a window all in one flight
become part of your past even the faces
of your best friends fade whether in love
or disregard and in five hours
all that is strange becomes merely different

you learn to love in another language
or with your arms tucked in
and all of a sudden you belong to no-one
and no-where belongs to you

Too many folks need thanks here for me not to forget a name somewhere, but to my partner who lets me be so many impossible people, and loves me anyway, Marty McConnell, Lynne Procope who holds me and has my back always as i will always have hers, Kwame Dawes who gave this a good hard look and who gave me invaluable mentorship, all of Cave Canem, without whom i might still be holding my breath. To the louderARTS Project crew from the top and beginning; Guy Gonzalez who pushed back all the time and often when we needed it most, Fish Boogie who represents hard all the time, Oscar Bermeo, Mara Jebsen who bends my mind often and Rich Villar and Emily "bad influence" Kagan and Rachel "roll hard" McKibbens and Raymond Daniel Medina and Abena "dkny" Koomson and Elana Bell and Eric Guerierri who is still a jackass; and compatriot poet who made me comfortable with my own peculiar voice in poetry, Cheryl Boyce-Taylor, and Peter Conti (R.I.P.) and Marty and Lynne again, and every single person with whom i've ever been on a slam team. Big up to Bassey and Ishle and Tai Freedom. To Patrick Rosal, who has been an immediate brother and confidant and friend, Kevin Coval who continues to build with, and challenge me. To Quraysh Ali Lansana who believes and loves and Jerry Quickley who believes and loves. To Samantha Thornhill who is smarter and more forgiving and loving than i think is possible sometimes. To Kristine Gotilla, whose art continues to teach me. To Toni Asante Lightfoot.

To VisionIntoArt and all that it has forced me to consider about being an artist and for all the belief in my work, even when i wasn't so sure. Paola, i love you huge, and Nora, thank you so much, and Holter and Pablo and Erik and Nadia and Lynne again. Milica Paranosic for being so intense and doing all this work with all this passion and love.

To Bar 13, Thomas Sullivan and the world's best bartender, Maureen. To Sam Reynolds, the best roommate ever!

To Maureen Benson and all that we will change and build and the H. To Geoff Trenchard and the H. To Hallie Hobson and the H.

To Andi Strickland.

To all of Queen's Royal College, especially Larry and Barrington and Cyril (with whom i stood in the cafeteria and insulted people all lunch time long) and Rick and Gary and Dave and Sheldon and Lenny and Shoogar. In particular to my principal Winston Douglas who drove home that "(my) responsibility is clear. Be a man." To present principal Bill Carter and to all the teachers who got through to me despite my own best efforts.

To Hunter College and the Student Liberation Action committee and especially Kahil. To Professor Root and Suheir Hammad and Professors Payne and Kinyatti for teaching me about the Mau Mau.

To Marcia Mark. To The Lydian Singers Choir.
Staceyann Chin with whom i honed so much and laugh so long and argue so much and share such love and drama. To the National Poetry Slam for giving me so many stages and such a forum and to the folks who've taught me there like Daphne Gottlieb and Arianna Waynes (who answer all my alternative sexuality questions) and Glenis Redmond and Jason Carney and Regie Gibson and Cass King and her costume closet and Karen Finneyfrock and her costume closet, "Big Booty" and butterfly house poems and Wammo and Danny Solis and Marc Smith. To Gabrielle. To Keith Roach for opportunity and a font of jazz music stories. To unarguably, the fiercest slammer ever, and if you young slam folks don't know who your BabeRuthMichaelJordanJimBrownPele is, it's Patricia Smith and she can still hurt you! To Kalamu ya Salaam and Amiri Baraka who taught me about integrity and honesty, and over time, why they were so worried about this slam thing. To the fact that they were right. To Willie Perdomo who gave me real advice when he didn't have to and Colin Channer who reconnected me to many of the Caribbean stories we share. To Saul Williams who told me to risk looking foolish and Beau Sia who takes that risk and makes it into beautiful art.

To the Spring Lounge. To Reservoir.

To Urban Word and the family that has become. To Jeff Kass and Volume and the amazing writers continuing to be produced there. To Salome Mohajer-Ganjei and her intent to teach and teach well and being well on her way there. To Donna Strange and Kali Handelman.

To Greg Polvere and Global Talent Associates; and Jay Love for booking me first.

To the Domino Effect, Lynne again and Veronica and Jamaal. Neisha Jadoonan who represented and supported hard, time and time again. To Sherry Ann Smith who gave me a hard as hell time when i was president of the drama club in 1985 and took me to my first poetry reading in Brooklyn in 1994; it's all your fault. To Cherrie Campbell and all we share so intensely and to vaasna ka jaadu. To the Hunter Organization of Trinidad and Tobago Students (yes, HOTTS) and Allison, Ron, Ian, Renee, Joanne, Rhonda, Liesl, Natasha, Paula and Gavin for all the evenings within "the establishment". To Brian Colthrust for all the stories we've made up that aren't poems... yet, and for everything we've got away with...so far.

To the Perez boys, Andy, Ancil, and in particular, Anthony, who many miles away continues to be "the one", my protector and best friend forever. To Cleo for representing for the rest of Arouca and feeding me.

To Paula who wrestled with me and fought me and laughed with me for years. To old family and the new, the ones who've given me renewed purpose and new understanding of what family can mean, Wole and Ayanbi, i love you. To my step-father Rawle Agard who gave me his name and offered to adopt me and my father Roosevelt John Williams whom i am beginning to know and understand and love.

To every student i have ever taught. To every student i have ever not reached. To every student who has reached me.

To every single person who has ever believed in me, loved me, booked me for a show, given me an edit or cheered me on without saying a word, i love you and need you and appreciate you deeply; for real, for real.

Roger Bonair-Agard was born and raised in Trinidad. A Cave Canem fellow, he is the co-author of Burning Down the House and his poetry has appeared in numerous anthologies and publications. He is a two-time National Slam Champion and performs his work in front of national and international audiences. The co-founder of the louderARTS Project, he co-curates its reading series at Bar 13 in New York City. He lives in Brooklyn, New York.

CD Listing

1   Introduction
2   cane brulee*
3   chantuel hymns
4   The devil in music
5   Bullet Points
6   1981
7   The mandate
8   photo graph
9   1986
10   Bird Watching
11   weusi alphabeti
12   song for trent lott
13   truth applies for a green card
14   the sadness of migration
15   blue sex prodigy

16   Introduction to live reading in Munich, Germany
17   weusi alphabeti
18   in the same breath as my father
19   hw the ghetto loves us back
20   love rev 2
21   naming and other Christian things

music and production: Celena Glenn
except *music and production: Milica Paranosic